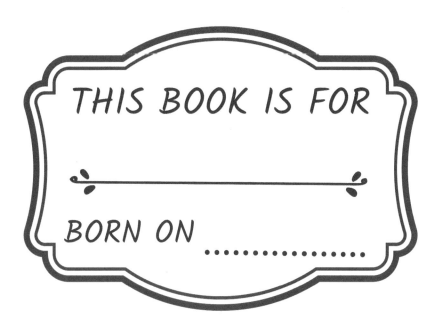

THIS BOOK IS FOR

BORN ON

WITH LOTS OF LOVE FROM

Forever & Always

Some things are infinite. There's no biggest number, no farthest star, no end to my love for you.

The day I found out we were expecting you, I felt...

DATE _____

_____

_____

_____

_____

_____

_____

_____

_____

_____

_____

_____

_____

_____

My hopes for you are...

DATE _____

_____

_____

_____

_____

_____

_____

_____

_____

_____

_____

_____

_____

_____

_____

_____

_____

I'm overjoyed to be a mother/father because...

DATE _____

_____

_____

_____

_____

_____

_____

_____

_____

_____

_____

_____

_____

_____

_____

_____

_____

As a parent, I hope to...

DATE _____

_____

_____

_____

_____

_____

_____

_____

_____

_____

_____

_____

_____

_____

_____

During pregnancy, life was like this...

DATE _____

_____

_____

_____

_____

_____

_____

_____

_____

_____

_____

_____

_____

_____

While you were in the womb, we bonded with you in this way...

DATE _____

_____

_____

_____

_____

_____

_____

_____

_____

_____

_____

_____

_____

_____

_____

_____

While you were in the womb, these major things happened in the family...

DATE _____

_____

_____

_____

_____

_____

_____

_____

_____

_____

_____

_____

_____

_____

While you were in the womb, we did these types of things each day...

DATE _____

While you were in the womb, we had some fascinating adventures together, like...

DATE _____

_____

_____

_____

_____

_____

_____

_____

_____

_____

_____

_____

_____

_____

_____

While you were in the womb, you were like this...

DATE _____

_____

_____

_____

_____

_____

_____

_____

_____

_____

_____

_____

_____

_____

_____

When we found out we were having a girl, I felt...

DATE _____

Before you were even born, I loved you because...

DATE _____

_____

_____

_____

_____

_____

_____

_____

_____

_____

_____

_____

_____

_____

On the day you were born...

DATE _____

_____

_____

_____

_____

_____

_____

_____

_____

_____

_____

_____

_____

_____

Your first home was...

_____

_____

_____

_____

_____

_____

_____

_____

_____

_____

_____

_____

_____

_____

Here are the best memories when you were a baby....

DATE _____

_____

_____

_____

_____

_____

_____

_____

_____

_____

_____

_____

_____

_____

_____

The weirdest thing you did when you were a baby...

DATE _____

_____

_____

_____

_____

_____

_____

_____

_____

_____

_____

_____

_____

_____

_____

Here are a few things you should know about our family...

DATE _____

_____

_____

_____

_____

_____

_____

_____

_____

_____

_____

_____

_____

_____

Here are a few things you should know about me...

DATE _____

_____

_____

_____

_____

_____

_____

_____

_____

_____

_____

_____

_____

_____

_____

_____

You're so fortunate to be born into this family because...

DATE _____

My favorite part of being a parent...

DATE _____

_____

_____

_____

_____

_____

_____

_____

_____

_____

_____

_____

_____

_____

_____

The hardest thing about being a parent...

DATE _____

The most rewarding thing about parenting you...

DATE _____

_____

_____

_____

_____

_____

_____

_____

_____

_____

_____

_____

_____

_____

When you are older, I hope you know that...

DATE _____

_____

_____

_____

_____

_____

_____

_____

_____

_____

_____

_____

_____

_____

_____

Congratulations on your achievements...

DATE _____

Here's a story I'd like to share with you...

DATE _____

_____

_____

_____

_____

_____

_____

_____

_____

_____

_____

_____

_____

_____

I promise to...

DATE _____

_____

_____

_____

_____

_____

_____

_____

_____

_____

_____

_____

_____

_____

_____

_____

Someday, I hope you will...

_____

_____

_____

_____

_____

_____

_____

_____

_____

_____

_____

_____

_____

_____

_____

I hope you grow up in a word that is...

DATE _____

_____

_____

_____

_____

_____

_____

_____

_____

_____

_____

_____

_____

_____

_____

I want to apologize for...

DATE _____

_____

_____

_____

_____

_____

_____

_____

_____

_____

_____

_____

_____

_____

_____

_____

Someday, I hope we do this together...

DATE _____

_____

_____

_____

_____

_____

_____

_____

_____

_____

_____

_____

_____

_____

_____

_____

_____

_____

One thing that I'm most grateful for...

DATE _____

Forgive me for...

DATE _____

_____

_____

_____

_____

_____

_____

_____

_____

_____

_____

_____

_____

_____

_____

The most significant thing that I've learned from life so far...

DATE _____

_____

_____

_____

_____

_____

_____

_____

_____

_____

_____

_____

_____

_____

I love you from the bottom of my heart...

DATE _____

_____

_____

_____

_____

_____

_____

_____

_____

_____

_____

_____

_____

_____

_____

_____

I believe in you, here's why ...

_____

_____

_____

_____

_____

_____

_____

_____

_____

_____

_____

_____

_____

_____

I think you're beautiful both inside and out...

DATE _____

_____

_____

_____

_____

_____

_____

_____

_____

_____

_____

_____

_____

_____

_____

You make me proud to a great extent...

DATE _____

I'd like you to know what my treasures are...

DATE _____

_____

_____

_____

_____

_____

_____

_____

_____

_____

_____

_____

_____

_____

_____

_____

Don't ever settle for second best because...

DATE _____

_____

_____

_____

_____

_____

_____

_____

_____

_____

_____

_____

_____

_____

Sometimes my love makes me afraid when...

DATE _____

_____

_____

_____

_____

_____

_____

_____

_____

_____

_____

_____

_____

_____

_____

You can always come to me—no matter what—I will be here for you...

DATE _____

_____

_____

_____

_____

_____

_____

_____

_____

_____

_____

_____

_____

_____

_____

I want you to listen to my heart...

DATE _____

Just to Note

DATE _____

_____

_____

_____

_____

_____

_____

_____

_____

Just to Note

DATE _____

_____

_____

_____

_____

_____

_____

_____

Just to Note

_____

_____

_____

_____

_____

_____

_____

Just to Note

_____

_____

_____

_____

_____

_____

_____

Just to Note

DATE _____

_____

_____

_____

_____

_____

_____

_____

Just to Note

DATE _____

_____

_____

_____

_____

_____

_____

_____

Just to Note

DATE _____

_____

_____

_____

_____

_____

_____

_____

Just to Note

DATE _____

_____

_____

_____

_____

_____

_____

_____

Just to Note

DATE _____

_____

_____

_____

_____

_____

_____

_____

Just to Note

DATE _____

_____

_____

_____

_____

_____

_____

_____

Just to Note

DATE _____

_____

_____

_____

_____

_____

_____

_____

Just to Note

DATE _____

_____

_____

_____

_____

_____

_____

_____

Just to Note

DATE _____

_____

_____

_____

_____

_____

_____

_____

Just to Note

DATE _____

_____

_____

_____

_____

_____

_____

_____

Just to Note

DATE _____

_____
_____
_____
_____
_____
_____
_____

Just to Note

DATE _____

_____
_____
_____
_____
_____
_____
_____

Just to Note

DATE _____

_____

_____

_____

_____

_____

_____

_____

Just to Note

DATE _____

_____

_____

_____

_____

_____

_____

_____

Just to Note

DATE _____

_____

_____

_____

_____

_____

_____

_____

Just to Note

DATE _____

_____

_____

_____

_____

_____

_____

_____

Just to Note

DATE _____

_____

_____

_____

_____

_____

_____

_____

Just to Note

DATE _____

_____

_____

_____

_____

_____

_____

_____

Just to Note

DATE _____

_____

_____

_____

_____

_____

_____

_____

Just to Note

DATE _____

_____

_____

_____

_____

_____

_____

_____

Just to Note

DATE _____

_____

_____

_____

_____

_____

_____

_____

Just to Note

DATE _____

_____

_____

_____

_____

_____

_____

_____

Just to Note

DATE _____

_____

_____

_____

_____

_____

_____

Just to Note

DATE _____

_____

_____

_____

_____

_____

_____

Just to Note

DATE _____

_____

_____

_____

_____

_____

_____

_____

Just to Note

DATE _____

_____

_____

_____

_____

_____

_____

_____

Just to Note

DATE _____

_____

_____

_____

_____

_____

_____

_____

Just to Note

DATE _____

_____

_____

_____

_____

_____

_____

_____

Just to Note

DATE _____

_____

_____

_____

_____

_____

_____

_____

Just to Note

DATE _____

_____

_____

_____

_____

_____

_____

_____

Made in United States
Troutdale, OR
10/08/2023

13485694R00070